The Basic Essentials of
SNOWBOARDING

by John McMullen

D1456773

ICS BOOKS, Inc.
Merrillville, Indiana

THE BASIC ESSENTIALS OF SNOWBOARDING
Copyright © 1991 John McMullen

10 9 8 7 6 5 4 3 2 1

Printed in U.S.A.

DEDICATION

This book is dedicated to my mother who always told me I could do anything if I put my mind to it and to my fiance Cathy Carlisle for her help and support while I worked through all our weekends together.

ACKNOWLEDGEMENT

I would like to thank my high school art teachers Mr. Downey and Mr. Ken Piene for their guidance and Bonnie and Jim for turning me on to the sport of snowboarding.

Published by:
ICS Books, Inc.
One Tower Plaza
107 E. 89th Avenue
Merrillville, IN 46410
800-541-7323

Library of Congress Cataloging-in-Publication Data

McMullen, John, 1958–
 The basic essentials of snowboarding / by John McMullen.
  p.   cm. -- (The Basic essentials series)
 Includes index.
 ISBN 0-934802-77-7 : $4.95
 1. Snowboarding.   I. Title.   II. Series.
GV857.S57M37 1991   91-21207
796.9--dc20   CIP

TABLE OF CONTENTS

There is no room for error in the backcountry!

INTRODUCTION

As I stand on the edge of the ridge, the view of the mountains bathed in an alpine glow is spectacular. A gust of wind blows a wave of snow up and over the corniced edge. Looking down, I feel the depths of the couloir pulling me. My heart pounds with the surge of adrenalin.

An invigorating day of climbing steep sections of ice and rock have brought me to the top of the run, a gorge cutting into the face of the mountain. Today the conditions are good. In the summer this couloir is only five feet wide in some places, but now it is filled with solid, stable snow.

I plan to descend this route on a snowboard. My concentration and balance must be perfect. A fall could send me plummeting a thousand feet or more down the mountain. Visualizing the turns and jumps, I picture the perfect, flawless run.

My partner and I pull out our Pieps radios and check their operation. If one of us should get caught in an avalanche, the Pieps signal may be our only chance for survival.

I slip my snowboard out of the pack—a modern sled, made only for the purpose of going down hills *fast*. On flat ground it would be like a fish out of water. I step into the plate binding, clipping it securely to my boots, and slide to the edge of the abyss. I'm amped and ready to rage.

Raising my arms, as if to fly, I tip the nose of my board over the edge. The slope is steep and the snow is hard and fast. Rock outcrops flash in front of my face. Centering myself and compressing, I lean forward into a frontside turn to slow my speed. As I ride up onto the sidewall of the couloir, I lean back on my heels, swinging my front arm back over the nose of the board, initiating a backside turn. The snow flies from the bottom of my board in a feathery rooster tail.

Carving turns to control my speed I shred my way down the seemingly endless pipe. Suddenly I see a rise in front of me, and as I hit the crest I find it is over a ledge. Completely airborne, I keep my weight forward and my arms up to maintain balance as I fly through the air. The powder below catches me and spits me out.

Ahead of me the run opens up. I see an awesome cornice formed on a ridge and head for it. Setting up to hit the face, I gain speed and race up the wall. It's steep and I slow down, but not before I leave the top. In the air I twist, planting my hand on the lip, and turn to slide back down the face. Leaning back on my board, I float over the steep powder.

My partner catches up with me as we hit the tree line. We carve turns through groves of aspen, pine, and spruce. Between the shadows the sun reflects off the snow like millions of tiny mirrors. Another beautiful day of boarding. I can't wait until tomorrow.

I often wonder if the inventor of the snowboard ever imagined that the sport would develop into what it is today: the extreme descents, the radical maneuvers in the halfpipe, and the speed now attainable in the slalom and downhill.

1. HISTORY AND DEVELOPMENT OF THE SNOWBOARD

From Snurfer to Snowboard

The first snowboards were made by Jem in the late 1960s. The Snurfer board consisted of a board, larger than a skateboard, with a slightly upturned nose and a rope attached through it. The surface of the board was covered with staples so the rider's boots could get purchase on the board. These Snurfer boards were difficult to control but fun to ride.

It took many years before the snowboard saw a great deal of change in design. In 1979, Jake Burton Carpenter showed up at a contest with a new board that he had designed. The Burton board was longer and wider than the Snurfer and had the addition of bungie boot bindings. The bindings were set at an angle comparable to the stance used on a skateboard. This allowed faster rides and tricks to be performed with more control. It took a couple of years for the bindings to gain popularity, but soon they became standard equipment on all snowboards.

New board and binding designs soon followed. One of these new designs was the Winterstick. This board had many design features that made it popular. Bigger than the Snurfer board it had a radical shape that allowed better turning control, and a wide nose enabled it to float easily over deep snow. Many Wintersticks are still in use.

Now, many ski manufacturers and independent designers are making snowboards. New developments in surface materials, core materials, and shaping are being discovered every day.

Figure 1-1   The Snurfer snowboard   **Figure 1-3**   An Asymmetrical snowboard

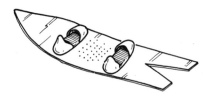

Figure 1-2   The Winterstick snowboard

One of the most radical new shapes—the asymmetrical snowboard—has a shifted sidecut that enables a rider to turn easily in either direction with much less effort than with a standard board. Most asymmetrical boards have been designed for alpine or slalom riding, but new designs for freeriding are currently being developed. The latest snowboard designs include very high-tech surface materials, such as Kevlar. They also include radical sidecut radii for improved turn control and a wide variety of flex patterns and lengths.

Another piece of equipment that has seen some development is the snowboarding boot. Sorel and some other boot manufacturers are now making boots especially designed for snowboarding. The new designs feature heavy-duty construction and innerboots that are warmer and add more support to the ankle area. Another new design is the hard-bottom and soft-top boot. This type of boot offers the lower foot the comfort of the hard boot and the flexibility of the soft boot.

The latest development in boots is the hard boot, which is much like a ski boot but more flexible. This boot uses a step-in plate binding, which attaches to the front and back welts of the boot. These new boots are the ultimate in warmth and comfort. Hard boots give an incredible amount of turning and edge control. They are the choice of most alpine, slalom, and extreme backcountry riders.

Snowboarding Competition

Competitive snowboarding started soon after the first snowboards were made. Originally, they were put on mostly for fun and they gave the few riders that were around the chance to see each other's tricks and to learn new ones.

With the improvements in snowboarding equipment, the number of riders grew. To advertise their products, ski resorts, manufacturers, and clothing companies began to sponsor competitions and riders. Presently, competitions are held at many ski resorts and riders can compete in freestyle, slalom, downhill and halfpipe events. There are competitions for both men and women, and often there are categories specially for the younger and older riders.

In a freestyle competition a snowboarder is judged on creativity and difficulty of the tricks performed. This type of competition is held on a mogul run with lots of bumps and jumps.

Snowboarders also compete in slalom races. Speed and accuracy are the elements of this type of competition.

The downhill is the traditional race. It is held on a long, steep, smooth course, and the rider with the fastest time wins.

Halfpipe competitions are very dynamic. Usually man-made, a competition halfpipe is shaped like a pipe that is cut in half lengthwise and is slightly tilted to one end. The rider drops into the pipe on the upper end and performs tricks off of the walls of the pipe. Expert riders often fly up into the air to perform their tricks, which is very exciting to watch. Riders are judged on their creativity and the difficulty of the tricks.

It is now possible to snowboard at almost all ski resorts in the world. By buying a regular ski pass at a resort you can ride the lift to the top of some of the best hills in the world for the shred of your life. Snowboarding at resorts is great fun. Runs of all levels of difficulty are available for the beginner to the expert boarder, and some resorts have built a halfpipe for the freestyle enthusiast.

Backcountry Snowboarding

Backcountry snowboarding has become very popular. This type of snowboarding takes place in undeveloped mountainous areas where the rider must Snowcat, ski, hike, and sometimes climb to get to the top of the desired run. Often the areas are only accessible by helicopter.

The kind of snowboarding requires extensive knowledge of wilderness survival. Understanding weather and snow conditions and having the proper gear are essential. From Alaska to Patagonia, from the Matterhorn to Mount Kilimanjoro, one will find serious descents down the steepest, highest mountains in the world. Snowboarders have climbed mountains and made descents that would make your hair stand on end.

2. HOW TO PICK A SNOWBOARD

The sport of snowboarding requires very little equipment. A snowboard, warm high-top boots, eye protection, and warm clothing is about all you will need.

Figure 2-1   Choosing a snowboard can be confusing if you don't know where or what type of riding you want to do.

5

The base of this equipment is the snowboard. A close relative of the snow ski, the snowboard is constructed much like it, but is wider to accommodate a sideways stance on the board. The variety of snowboards has grown significantly in the last few years. Most manufacturers are coming out with boards designed for specific styles of riding, and freestyle, alpine, halfpipe, and racing boards are now available in many lengths and widths.

Snowboard Construction

A snowboard is constructed of many materials sandwiched together. The deck, shell, core, and base are surrounded by the sidewalls and edges. The different types of construction vary considerably from one manufacturer to the next, and new combinations are still being developed.

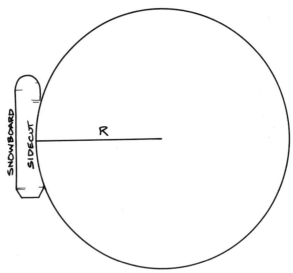

Figure 2-2a   Side cut radius

The Deck

The deck, or top of the board and the sidewalls are often made of plastic, or ABS, which is a durable, and scratch-resistant plastic, that is strong and easy to silk screen.

The Core

The core of the board is wood or polyurethane. The wood laminate core comes in two configurations: vertical or horizontal. Vertical construction is very desirable. The side-by-side arrange-

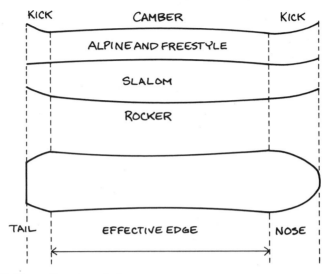

Figure 2-2b   Snowboard shapes

ment across the board gives the board more vertical rigidity, making it stronger and more springy. Horizontal laminates have several drawbacks and are consequently used by few manufacturers. Other materials are often added to wood-core construction to improve the board's characteristics and handling.

Polyurethane cores, or foam cores, are commonly used because of their low cost and durability. They are very responsive and cost less than a board with a wood core.

The newest type of core construction is the honeycomb. Built of aluminum or other super-light materials, this type of core offers the strength of wood and the lightness of foam.

The Shell and Other Construction Materials

Foam and honeycomb cores are covered with a shell. This shell can be made of several different materials, such as aluminum, fiberglass, carbon fiber graphite, or Kevlar.

Fiberglass is a preferred shell material because of its light weight, high strength, low cost, and manufacturing simplicity. It is produced in three forms: cloth, preimpregnated, or precured.

Aluminum is stronger and livelier than fiberglass, it provides better dampening, which reduces the amount of chatter and vibration in the board.

Carbon fiber graphite (CFG) is similar to fiberglass. It is manufactured in cloth form, is very strong, and offers great damping properties. It has a greater tensile strength (it stretches) than Kevlar, and not much is needed to change the flex of a board.

Kevlar is an aramid fiber that is light and strong and provides good damping, but it is more expensive than carbon fiber graphite.

Rubber is used as a damping material in some snowboards. All of these core types are suitable for the beginner to the advanced rider.

Base Grades

The base of the board is made of polyethylene. This material comes in different grades: Extruded polyethylene, cheapest type of base, is melted and pushed through a slot to form a base material. UHMW, or ultrahigh-molecular-weight material is another type of base-grade polyethylene that can be extruded.

The best way to make a base is by sintering. This is done by taking a piece of extruded polyethylene and grinding it into very fine particles. The powder is then pressed into a cake and heated—sintered—to form a solid base that is still porous. The cake is sliced to form the base, then put on the board. The sintered base is very durable. It absorbs and holds wax easily and longer than an extruded base, and the speed is considerably greater.

A new type of base is the carbon-filled sintered polyethylene material. In most snow, especially wet conditions, it is faster than a clear base. It's not proven, but this could be because of the carbon's electrical conductivity, which reduces the buildup of static electricity.

The Edge

Most snowboards have metal edges. If you intend to ride at a ski resort, you will need metal edges on your board.

Some boards have cracked edges. These cracks isolate vibration and eliminate the stiffness of a continuous edge. Some boards have cracked or segmented edges only in the tip or tail.

Snowboards generally have a beveled edge, which helps initiate the turn. They are common on freestyle boards.

Snowboard Shape

Nose and Tail Kick

There are several important features that will determine the performance of a board. The nose, or front, of the board is turned up. This is called the nose kick. The back, or tail, of the board will also have some kick. Freestyle and alpine boards have more nose kick and tail kick than slalom boards. This is so you can ride backwards while freeriding.

Effective Edge

The amount of edge contact the board has is important. The effective edge runs from the nose kick to the tail kick. Short edge contact is good for "turnability" but not for high speeds or carving on hard snow.

Flex and Camber

Flex and camber determine a snowboard's stiffness and maneuverability. For a beginner, a board with an easy flex will soften landings and be easier to turn. A stiff board will accelerate out of a turn much faster and therefore will be better for racing or cruising. Most riders prefer an average flex pattern, which cushions landings and also gives good acceleration.

A board's camber is the amount of bow in the board when it is lying flat. Camber controls the amount of pressure distributed along the board's edge. Freestyle riders and beginners will want a board with low camber, while a cruiser or slalom rider will want a high camber. A negative camber means that the board is prebent in the opposite direction. This type of board is a "rocker."

Sidecut

The board's shape is determined by the sidecut. The radius of the board's sidecut relates directly to the turning radius of the snowboard. On most snowboards the sidecut is part of a circle. It's important to know the sidecut radius of the board. This allows you to compare the performance of a board of one length to a board that is longer or shorter.

An extreme sidecut gives more edge control and allows the rider to do tighter turns. Less sidecut reduces the amount of holding power on the tip and tail and, therefore is better for the beginner. The rider is less likely to catch their edge.

There are several types of sidecuts. The most common is a radial sidecut, which is a section of a circle and is constant throughout its entire length. The other types—elliptical, quadratic, and progressive—are more commonly used on specialized boards for downhill and slalom racing.

Picking Out Your Snowboard

For the beginner it's important to get a board that will allow you to ride "fakie" (backwards). A freestyle or alpine board with a little tail kick will do nicely. Also, check the flex of the board. You will want a board that is soft—that is, with a lot of flex. It's not necessary to go out and buy an expensive board; you can find many good deals on used equipment if you look.

There are three basic questions to answer when choosing a snowboard. First, where are you going to ride? Will you be riding on small hills in your back yard, boarding at a ski resort, heading for the backcountry, or possibly competing in a race or halfpipe event?

If you are not really sure how serious you are about the sport, get a simple alpine or freestyle board. It won't matter if it's an old model or not, you will still have fun.

If you plan to ride at a resort, you will need a board that has metal edges, strong bindings and a leash. An alpine board will do for regular riding, but, if you intend to ride in a halfpipe you might want a more specialized board.

Alpine boards are designed for cruising, powder, or mogul riding. And while they can be used in the halfpipe, they will not perform as well as a freestyle board because of their stiff flex pattern and high camber.

The freestyle board has more flex, lower camber, deeper sidecut, and a more pronounced nose and tail kick. There are several designs available and the choice is personal. However, if you are going to race slalom, there are boards specifically designed for this type of riding. Slalom boards are long with very stiff flex patterns, high camber, and radical sidecuts. Many slalom racers ride asymmetrical boards. The offset sidecut of the asymmetrical board makes it easier to turn backside, with less loss of speed.

Backcountry riders want strong, heavy-duty equipment. This might put some stress on your budget, but the high cost of gear will be worth it, especially if your life depends upon it. A strong but light board is needed and a board constructed of carbon fiber graphite or Kevlar is just that. Plate bindings and hard boots are preferred. Plate bindings are not bulky and they slide easily into and out of a pack. Hard boots are very warm and can be worn with crampons for difficult climbing on icy slopes. Together, they give excellent control for alpine riding.

Look at the equipment that riders you emulate use. They will often help you select the proper equipment.

The second question is, how big are your feet? A board's width should be as narrow as possible; however, your feet shouldn't extend over the edge of the board. If your feet are hanging over the edge, you will not be able to turn your board effectively. If you find a board you like but it is too narrow, you may have to adjust your stance.

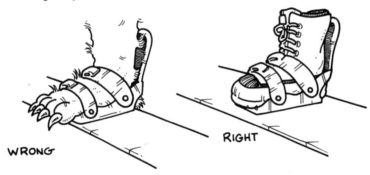

WRONG   RIGHT

Figure 2-3   The boards width should be as wide or wider than the length of your feet.

Third, how much do you weigh? Younger riders clearly need shorter equipment, but for most people over one hundred pounds the question is not one of length but of flex and camber. Your board's length should be determined by where you ride and the kinds of turns you make.

If your usage dictates the use of a 175 centimeter slalom board, then your weight will decide how stiff it should be. Lighter riders need softer boards; heavy riders need stiffer boards. The faster you ride, the stiffer the board should be to compensate for the increased force generated during turns.

A factor closely related to weight is rider height. In general, taller riders should use longer boards in their category because of their greater leverage.

Manufacturers offer a variety of boards in different lengths, but they do not offer boards with different flex patterns to match riders of various weights. However, the great diversity of products now on the market allows us to approximate the same effect through comparison shopping.

It might take you a couple of seasons to pick the best board for you. And with the sport developing so fast, you might end up selling your board after every season just to keep up with the technology.

3. TUNING YOUR SNOWBOARD

It's important to keep your board tuned *all season.* It will perform better if you do.

Different styles of riding require different tuning techniques. If you are planning to ride in a slalom race, you will want your edges very sharp. A freestyle rider might want his edges a little dull so spins can be performed without catching an edge. The air temperature will determine the type of wax you will use. Some manufacturers are now producing waxes designed specifically for snowboards. These are basically the same waxes used by downhill skiers, but they come in larger cakes to cover the large area required by the snowboard.

If you don't want to take your board to a professional ski tuner, you will need to get the following tools and supplies to do it yourself:

Swix wax remover
Rags
P-Tex sticks
Matches
Propane torch
Metal ski scraper
Small fine-toothed file

Ski edge file hold
Scotch base pad
Ski waxes
Long plastic scraper
Waxing iron
Phillips screwdriver

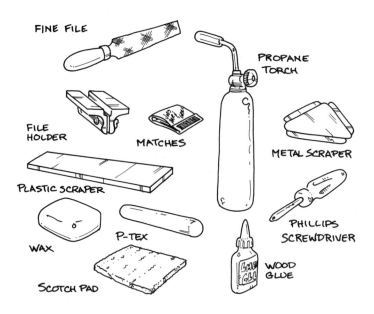

Figure 3-1   Snowboard tuning tools

Tuning

First you will need to clean the old wax off of your board base. Use some Swix wax remover and a clean rag. If you have any deep cuts in the base of your board, you will need to get some P-Tex, polyurethane, the same material that the snowboards base is made of. It comes in small sticks, so if the damage to your base is severe, you may need a couple of sticks. The P-Tex needs to be lit. Its ignition temperature is high, so a propane torch is needed.

Once you have the P-Tex lit, try to keep the flame pointing down. This will keep the carbon (black stuff) out of the P-Tex as it drips into the cuts. Apply sparingly to the cut and let it cool. When it is cool to the touch, use a metal scraper to smooth the excess P-Tex. You can then smooth the entire base with a Scotch base pad.

To sharpen your edges, use a *fine* file and file holder. The effective edge is all that needs sharpening. Use long, smooth strokes and not too much pressure. You don't want to file metal off, just sharpen what is there.

Now choose the wax that best suits the temperature you will be riding in. Use a wax iron to melt the wax, and drip it on the board. Starting at the widest part of the nose, drip wax down one third of the length of the board. Smooth out the wax with the iron, leaving a smooth, even coat on the section being waxed. With a wide, plastic wax scraper, smoothly scrape the wax towards the tail of the board. Leave the excess wax on the next area to be done and add wax if necessary. Repeat this until you reach the widest part of the tail. It is not necessary to wax the tip or tail of the board. If the wax is bumpy, you can smooth it with the Scotch pad.

Binding Check

Check your bindings for loose screws or missing parts prior to each use of the board. Use a Phillips screwdriver to check the screws holding your bindings to the board. If they are loose, take them out and apply a small amount of wood glue to the screw, then reinsert and tighten. Losing a binding while on the hill or in the backcountry could turn into a seriously dangerous situation.

4. OTHER SNOWBOARDING EQUIPMENT

Boots

After you find the right snowboard, you need to select your boots and bindings. A beginner can start with an inexpensive pair of Sorel-type boots. Get them a half size bigger than your street shoe size so you have good circulation and room for extra socks.

There are many new soft boots on the market today, and they are all pretty good. You will be wearing them for hours, so pick out a comfortable pair. Check out the construction and insulation carefully before making your choice.

Most freestyle and half-pipe riders prefer to wear soft boots because of their flexibility. The new hard-bottom, soft-top boot is very popular. This boot gives you the comfort of the hard boot, with the flexibility of the soft boot.

If you intend to ride in the backcountry or in alpine conditions, you might want to get hard boots. This type of boot will give more support for extreme moves on steep, hard ground. There are many different hard boots available. Look for one that is not too stiff in the upper, or that is adjustable.

Figure 4-1   Snowboarding boots

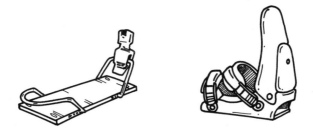

Figure 4-2   Snowboard bindings

Bindings

Soft boots need a soft binding. The soft binding usually has two or three quick-release buckles that hold the boot onto the board. The high back of the binding is there to give support while turning or doing tricks. A low-back soft binding is also available for use with hard boots.

Plate bindings are flat bindings with a bail at the front and back of the binding. The bails attach to the welt of the boot. They are very easy to get in and out of, and they are very strong. Plate bindings can be used only with hard boots. Choosing a binding and boot might take some trial and error before you find the best combination for your style of riding. Trying different bindings on rental snowboards is a good way to shop once you've decided on a boot.

The Leash

A snowboarding leash is a cord that connects the snowboard to the rider. One end of the leash is attached to the front binding and the other end is attached to the lower front leg of the rider. This cord's purpose is to serve as a backup should the front binding fail. All ski resorts require that a leash be worn at all times while on the hill. There are many different styles of leashes and the choice is personal. A simple piece of perlon cord will do in a pinch. I like the new locking design that allows you to lock your board easily to any pole or rack at a resort.

Clothing

Proper clothing is very important. As with many other outdoor activities, it's a good idea to layer your garments so you can dress down when you start warming up. Snowboarding requires freedom of movement, so BIG is the way to go. On cold days I will wear light Thermax or polypro socks with wool socks over them, Thermax or polypro pants (covered with fleece pants if it's really

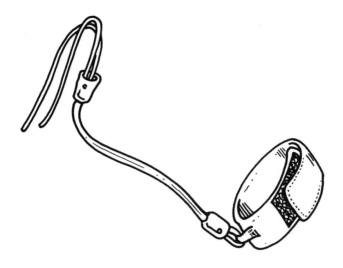

Figure 4-3   Deluxe snowboard leash (Any kind of cord will do.)

cold) and a baggy pair of waterproof pants, and a Thermax or polypro top with a T-shirt or sweatshirt and a big waterproof or water-resistant jacket.

Clothing choice is very personal. Keep in mind that, if you are going to crash a lot, you may want more protection. Snow can be very abrasive, so I would suggest that you stick with long-sleeve shirts until you have gained more experience.

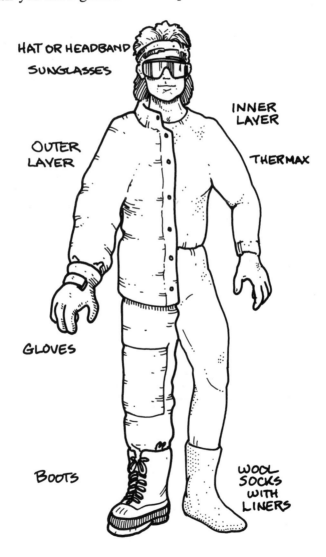

HAT OR HEADBAND

SUNGLASSES

INNER LAYER

OUTER LAYER

THERMAX

GLOVES

BOOTS

WOOL SOCKS WITH LINERS

Figure 4-4   Snowboarding clothing/layering

Eyewear

You should always wear some type of eye protection while snowboarding. Ultraviolet rays are extremely damaging to your eyes, and they are intensified in snowy conditions. Invest in a good pair of sunglasses or goggles. I prefer the wraparound style sunglasses, because they are light and allow me to use my peripheral vision. Sunglasses should be secured to you by a lanyard. Chums or Croakies will work. Goggles are great if the lens is large and doesn't restrict your visibility.

Skin Protection

Always wear a sunscreen with 15 SPF or more to protect your skin from harmful solar radiation, which is the leading cause of skin cancer.

5. BASIC SNOWBOARDING

Stretching

Now that you have the perfect board and all the gear necessary to hit the slopes, you're probably just itching to get into the your bindings and shred.

Well, I'm sure you've heard this one before, but as with most physically demanding sports, it's a good idea to do a session of stretching exercises before you go out for a hard day of boarding.

Stretching has many benefits for the athlete. It can optimize your learning, practice, and performance of skilled movements. It increases your ability to relax and think clearly. Most of all it can reduce the risk of joint sprain, muscle strain, and soreness. A stretching session gives you a chance to relax and to visualize yourself snowboarding effortlessly through the snow.

The following list of stretches is only a recommendation. There are hundreds of stretches that you can do. If you feel the stretch is too difficult or painful, don't do it.

Prestretching and Stretching Guidelines
1. Don't stretch immediately before eating.
2. Empty your bladder and bowels before you start stretching.

3. Do your stretching on a nonskid surface such as a padded carpet or firm mat, preferably in a quiet area.

4. Remember, when you stretch, don't bounce or force your body into position. Reach slowly and concentrate on relaxing the muscles you are stretching. Release each stretch as carefully as you went into it.

5. Breathing is an important aspect of each stretch; be conscious of your breathing. Accentuate your exhalation when moving deeper into a stretch.

Two Stretches are for the Posterior Lower Leg and Achilles Tendon.

1. Kneel down on the floor with your hands in front of you. Inhale and shift one foot forward, placing it flat on the floor. Exhale and lean forward onto your arms. Hold this stretch for a few seconds, then relax.

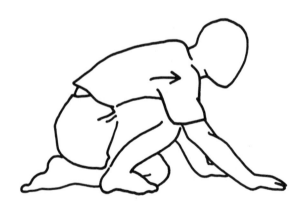

2. While standing, place both hands on your knees. Keep your heels flat on the floor and parallel. Exhale, then slowly flex

your knees, bringing them as close to the floor as possible. Hold
this stretch, then relax.

Back of the Knee

3. Sit on your mat upright with your legs straight in front of
you. Keep one leg straight and bend the other so its heel touches
the groin of your extended leg. Exhale, lean forward, and grasp

your foot. Keep your leg straight, and pull on your foot. Breathe
normally as you hold the stretch. Hold this stretch, then relax.

Upper Leg

4. Stand upright in front of an elevated platform. Slowly raise your leg and rest it on the platform. Exhale, keeping both legs straight and your hips squared. Extend your upper back and bend forward at the waist. Lower your trunk onto your raised thigh. Hold this stretch, then relax.

Adductors

5. Sit on the floor with your legs flexed and straddled and heels together. Hold your feet and ankles and pull them as close to your buttocks as possible. Exhale and lean forward from the hips

without bending your back. Lower your chest as close to the floor as possible. Hold this stretch, then relax.

Quadriceps

6. Stand upright with the top of one foot resting on a low stand or chair behind you. Exhale and flex your front knee. Hold this stretch, then relax.

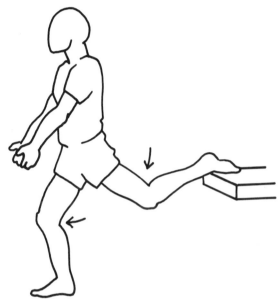

Buttocks and Hips

7. Lie on your back with your knees flexed and arms out to your sides. Exhale and lower both legs to the floor to one side while keeping your elbows, head, and shoulders flat on the floor. Hold this stretch, then relax.

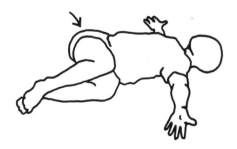

8. Sit on the floor with your legs extended in front of you and your hands resting on the floor behind your hips. Flex one leg across the other and slide your foot toward your buttocks. Keep

your foot flat on the floor. Reach over your flexed leg with the opposite arm and place your elbow on the outside of the flexed knee. Exhale, look over your shoulder in the direction you are turning your torso, and push back on your knee with your elbow. Hold this stretch, then relax.

9. Stand about four feet from a wall. Bend one leg, keeping the other leg straight, and rest your hands above your head on the

wall. Keep your back leg in a straight line with your upper body and your heel down, flat, and parallel to your hips. Exhale and slowly rotate your rear leg out sideways from the hip. Hold this stretch, then relax.

Abdomen and Hip Flexors

10. Kneel on the floor with your legs slightly apart and your toes pointing out behind you. Place your hands flat against your lower back and upper buttocks. Exhale and slowly arch your back,

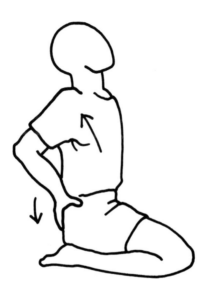

pushing your hips out in front of you and contracting your buttocks. Exhale and continue to arch backwards. Let your head drop back, open your mouth, and gradually slide your hands toward your heels. Hold this stretch, then relax.

Back and Trunk

11. **Warning: Don't do this one if you have knee or back problems.** Lie on your back with your hands to your sides, palms

down. Push down, raise your legs up into a squat position until your knees are close to your forehead. Slide your hands up to your lower back for support. Hold this stretch, then relax.

12. Kneel known on your mat with your arms reaching out in front of you as far as possible. Lower your chest to the floor.

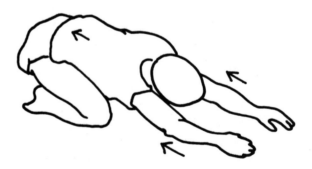

Exhale, twist your upper torso slightly, and press down with your palms and forearms on the floor. Hold this stretch, then relax.

This routine will take about twenty minutes if you do each stretch for thirty seconds. Stretching will not only benefit your performance snowboarding, it also will give you the flexibility to excel in all of your activities and an increased sense of well-being.

Getting into Your Bindings and onto the Lift

Skating

After stretching, go to a flat area near the beginner's lift and put on your front binding. It is easiest to do this while sitting. With your front binding on, stand up and get used to moving around on the flats.

One of the hardest things for the beginning snowboarder to get used to is the awkwardness of moving around on flat ground. Some beginners do fine coming down the hill, but once they take their back foot out of the binding they find they have no control.

If your board comes flying out from under you with every step on the flats, it's because you are pointing your front foot straight instead of the board straight. The base of your board should be flat on the show and pointed diagonally. Having your foot cocked at an angle is awkward, but with practice you will soon gain control and confidence.

With your rear foot free, bend your front leg, get low, and push from the toeside of the board. Rise up with each push, then put your rear foot on the board between the bindings. Balance completely on your front leg. Let the board slide as far as possible, then push again. Practice this until you develop a rhythm, keeping the board moving in a straight line.

Next, try skating with your rear foot off of the heelside of the board. Using smaller steps, push off and again put your back foot in the center of the deck and slide. Develop a smooth flow from one to the next.

Figure 5-1 Snowboarding skating

Once you get the two skates down, go to a flat area, begin from the toeside, get low, and push off. Release and step to the center of the board. Then get low again and push off from the heelside of the board, then back to center again. Practice until you find you can push from toeside to heelside alternately without putting your foot on the deck. Although it's difficult, this is a great exercise for balance.

When you master the skate you will be ready to get in the lift line and tackle your first run. But, first, you might want to practice skating to a stop on an easy slope. Most lifts have an exit slope below the chair as soon as you get to the top. It's important that you are able to control your direction and speed when getting off the chair—there are usually people hanging out at the top of a lift. Practice skating and stepping into the middle of your board, then coming to a controlled stop heelside and toeside before you get on the lift. It will save you considerable embarrassment and/or injury.

First-day Precautions

Before you get on the lift, I would like to recommend a couple of things that will make your first day of snowboarding more enjoyable. You will probably be spending quite a bit of time on the snow, sitting or crashing, so wear waterproof clothing. If you don't have waterproof gloves, you should have an extra pair of regular ones handy. When the snow is hardpack or ice, a pair of knee pads will save your knees from injury. Don't let your pride get in the way—you will probably be on your knees much of the day. Some snowboarding pants come with removable knee and butt pads built into them.

Now your ready to get on the lift.

Getting onto the Lift

All snowboarders have to wear a leash. This is a cord that connects the board to the rider so the board will not leave the rider should the binding fail. Make sure your leash is on. All ski areas require them to be worn while riding the lifts.

Step up to the line with both feet even and your board pointing straight ahead. If you are riding with a skier, be careful not to clack his ski as the lift picks you up. If the chair you are riding doesn't have a foot rest, you will find that sticking your toe under the back of your board will take some of the weight off of your other leg and make the ride much more enjoyable. Now, kick back and enjoy the scenery.

Figure 5-2   Resting the board on your toe while riding the lift will make the ride more comfortable.

Getting Off of the Lift

When you get to the top of the lift, get yourself into position to descend off of the chair. Point the board straight ahead and place your rear foot in the center of the board. When you reach the descent slope, lean forward into the slope and away from anyone else getting off of the chair. Use your rear foot in the center of the board to do either a heelside or toeside turn to a stop as soon as you are clear of the chair slope. Hanging your toe over the edge of the board will help slow you down. This will take some practice, but after a few runs you will be more comfortable with the move. Beware of ice patches when you get off of the chair.

After you get off of the lift, find a safe spot and put on your back binding. Try to find a spot that is out of the path of the other skiers getting off of the lift.

Your First Run

Start out on the beginners' slope. Your first day of snow-boarding will set the stage for a long enjoyable experience if you start slowly, so don't push yourself too hard.

The Fall Line

Skate to the top of the run, and look over the edge for the fall line. The fall line is the line that an object will naturally take when going down the slope. For instance, if you take a snowball and roll it down the hill, it will roll into the fall line.

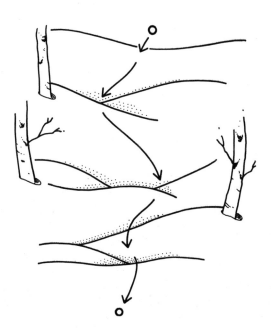

Figure 5-3   The fall line is the route that an object will naturally take when falling down a slope.

The Sideslip

The first basic maneuver you will need to learn to execute is called the sideslip. Sideslipping will build edge awareness and edge control.

Stand on the slope with your toe edge in the snow across from the fall line. If you find it hard to stand on the slope, kneel down. Practice going from the kneeling position to a standing position with your toe edge in the snow and your heel edge out of the snow. The proper stance is centered over the board with your knees slightly bent and your head and back straight. Your arms will be at your side. You should be looking straight ahead, not at your feet or the board.

Once you feel comfortable standing, slowly lower your heel edge towards the snow. This will release the toe edge and you will begin sliding in a controlled way down the slope. If you apply more weight to the front of the board, you will go forward; more weight to the back and you will sideslip backward. Look for a safe spot about thirty feet downhill from you and slide to that spot. Lift your heelside edge higher off the snow to stop. This is called the straight sideslip on the toe edge. Practice the sideslip forward and backward. Connect the two and descend by traversing the slope. Do a straight sideslip across the slope and then a reverse sideslip back to the other side.

Figure 5-4   Sideslip stance; look forward not down.

Next try the straight sideslip on the heel edge. Face forward with your toes pointing downhill and your board across the fall line. Slowly lower your toes until the board starts to move sideways down the hill. When you start to move, keep your speed smooth and constant by fine tuning your edge angle. Keep your eyes on the horizon to improve your balance, and try not to let your board get too flat on the slope. If it gets too flat, you will catch your downhill edge and go over onto your knees. Ouch!

Next add some directional control by shifting your weight. While in a sideslip, move some of your weight to the right foot and you will sideslip to the right. Center your weight onto your front foot to head sideways down the hill again. Then do the same thing but move to your left. Don't worry about the front or back of the board, just do it until you become comfortable in both directions. Keep your movements smooth and slow. It's a good idea to learn how to ride fakie (backwards) as it will come in handy later.

Turning

You will probably find that it is easier to turn your board to the frontside. This is because you are more inclined to lean forward onto your toeside edge than back onto your heelside edge. Get yourself pointed downhill. As you start gaining speed, keep your knees bent, lean forward onto your toeside edge, and apply some pressure. Keep your front arm up and your back arm bent into your body. Bring your front arm over the toeside edge. As the board turns, lift your heels to apply equal pressure to the front and back toeside edge. This will act as a brake. Don't follow the turn too far or you will spin and end up fakie. This is okay if you are ready for it. Just lean downhill and you will do another turn. Practice the frontside turn until you get it wired.

The backside turn is a bit tricky. Do your frontside turn, and when your board is pointing diagonally, flatten out the base and bring your front arm back over the board, as if you are opening a door. Your trailing arm should be bent into your torso. Keep your weight forward, knees bent, and apply pressure to your heelside edge by lifting your toes. Push your back foot out in front of you. Continue to ride your heelside edge until you are again traveling diagonally across the slope. To break, follow the turn until you are horizontal and apply pressure evenly to your heels. Practice your heelside turn until you feel comfortable, then try to connect the two—toeside turn to heelside turn. Remember to apply pressure to the edge as you initiate the turn. Get the whole edge into the action, and be aggressive.

Figure 5-5   Turning techniques:
Use your arms and upper body to initiate turns. Keep your knees bent.

Body Position

If you are cruising casually, your upper body will be in a high position. If you are being aggressive, you will be moving from the high position to a low position to get more pressure onto your edges.

Choosing a Line

Once you learn to connect your turns, you will start looking for a line down the slope. One of the greatest aspects of snowboarding is the ability to use the whole run. When you get to the bottom of the run, find a safe spot, out of traffic, and take off your back binding. You're now ready to get back on the lift and shred on another run.

Sketching, Falling, and Head Plants

Learning how to fall is another important aspect of snowboarding. Since the board is fixed to your boots and there is no release system, you must learn how to handle a crash without getting smacked in the face by your board or breaking your ankles, knees, or wrists.

TUCK THUMBS INTO PALMS

Figure 5-6   Falling roll: Tuck your thumbs into your palms.

The best way to prevent this is to be prepared. When you start to sketch (lose control), look below you for your landing area. Don't try to use the board as a brake—this could cause an instant face plant into the snow or whatever is below you. Instead, try to roll into the fall, using your leading shoulder.

Keep your arms in front of your chest and your thumbs tucked into your palms. If possible, bring your board over your body and try to land it in such a way that you can get back on top. You might actually have to jump into the fall in order to be in the correct position to recover. This takes quite a bit of practice, and it is easier to learn in powder.

6. INTERMEDIATE SNOWBOARDING

In this chapter I discuss techniques for the intermediate snowboarder and give a few suggestions to help you become a better rider. I suggest, however, that you take it slowly and learn all the basics before attempting any of the following maneuvers.

Ice, Crud, and Slush

Practice riding in different conditions. It's easy to get yourself dialed into a few good runs. You have every move wired but you aren't getting any better. If you force yourself to ride in terrain that is different, you will become a well-rounded rider.

Look for areas that other people avoid, like the crud along the sides of the run. On those hot days when the skiers are moaning about the slush, get out there and check it out. Snowboarding in slush is great! Icy hardpack is not as much fun to ride on, but you should learn how to handle it. You never know when you will hit a patch of ice. By riding in as many different conditions as possible you will force yourself to make the subtle adjustments required for each condition.

Choose Your Line

Choosing your line will also affect your riding. Be creative and select a line that uses the entire run. Observe all the features of

Figure 6-1   Choose the creative line.

the run and challenge yourself, no matter how easy the run might be.

Look for the outstanding features of the run. Be aware of bumps, jumps, and ledges. A fallen tree can be used for rail slides. Keep your eyes open and look for all the possibilities.

Boarding in the Trees

Boarding through the trees is killer fun, but be careful and don't board alone. If anything should happen to you or your board breaks, you could be in serious trouble. Watch out for branches, both hanging and below the snow. Wear sunglasses or goggles to protect your eyes. Take it easy when boarding through an area you are not familiar with. If you leave the designated resort run, be sure you are not in an out-of-bounds area.

Figure 6-2 Snowboarding through the trees is fun but dangerous. Always ride with a partner.

Timing

One of the most elusive skills to learn is timing—that is, the cadence or rhythm between turns. A good way to improve your timing is to follow riders who are better than you. Study their technique and position, not their style. Ask them to go slow so you can observe closely.

Turning on the Steeps

Jump turning on a steep slope is exhausting and difficult.

If you don't snowboard regularly, you might want to get in shape for this kind of riding.

Drops on a steep slope can be from three to more than six feet between turns. Most riders prefer using a short board for this kind of riding, one that will easily swing 180° Fahrenheit jumping from a standstill.

Start out on a moderately steep slope. Mental attitude is very important, so get psyched. Don't hold back. Be aggressive.

As you drop in, keep your board pointed slightly downhill. Immediately brake the board slightly by applying quick and firm

Figure 6-3   Riding steep bumps takes an aggressive attitude.

pressure to your uphill edge. As the edge reaches maximum bite on the slope, you will feel the force of the turn. Go with it, compressing slightly by bending at the knees, then spring up off the snow, swing the nose of the board through the fall line, and land the turn downhill.

This movement is repeated over and over until you reach the bottom of the slope. Always keep your torso, head, and arms facing in the direction of travel. It's best to keep your weight heavily over your front foot, using your back leg to pick up the tail and swing it through the turn. Resist the urge to lean into the wall, and stay on top of your board at all times.

Tricks

There are many tricks that can be done on a snowboard. Most of these will have some benefit for normal riding at resorts or in the backcountry.

Spins

The sliding 360-degree turn is fun. You probably have already done many spins while learning how to snowboard, but doing it with control is another skill.

It's easier to spin on a smooth, groomed slope. If you are in powder, you will need to get into the air to spin. Start by initiating a toeside turn, and don't carve too hard. When your board is perpendicular to the slope, lower your heels to flatten it out. Continue to push your back foot out behind you until the tail of your board is pointing down and you are riding fakie. Keep the base of your board flat. Lean back on your heels slightly (do not brake) and push your front foot out. Be careful to keep your weight on your heelside edge until the nose of your board is pointing downhill. Leaning forward too soon will cause you to catch your toeside edge, and the ensuing crash could be painful. The trick is to keep the base flat to the slope without putting too much pressure onto your lower edge.

Air

Catching "air" is one of the first tricks that snowboarders want to do. Getting into the air is usually not as hard as landing. If you have never tried it, here are some tips.

Figure 6-4   Catching "big air" in the halfpipe

Find a small mogul or bump to use as a jump. As you approach the jump, crouch slightly at the knees. Push off as you hit the top. Don't lean backward or too far forward while in the air. Keep your knees slightly bent until you are on the ground. They will absorb the force of the landing. Landing on your toeside edge, and carving a turn as you land, will help you control your speed as you land.

Another trick is the "half-cab." This involves catching air while riding fakie and executing a 180-degree spin. Approach a bump riding fakie. The trick is to kick off of the bump with the tail of your board as it hits the top of the bump and do a 180-degree spin in the air. Use your upper body momentum to spin your board around, and crouch as you land. Landing on your toeside edge will help you control the landing. Carve a toeside turn to check your speed. It's important to keep your body centered and straight. This trick takes a lot of practice, so start slowly and be careful. Snowboarding is an aggressive sport, but experience should be built slowly and safely.

Figure 6-5   A "half-cab" trick

After mastering these intermediate air moves you are ready to advance to the 360-degree air spin. I will describe only the basics of this trick because it is a difficult trick and should not be attempted without experience. It's a good idea to practice advanced tricks on a straight jump before attempting them in the halfpipe.

You will need a much larger mogul or jump to execute this trick. You need at least a three-foot air.

As you leave the top of the jump or pipe from your crouched position, you must use your upper body to get the spin initiated. Turn your head in the direction you want to spin. Also, drive your elbow in the same direction and pull the opposite elbow into your chest. Keep your body straight. Be sure to land the transition directly on top of the board with your weight centered. Don't forget to bend your knees before you land. There's not much advise to give on this one except to make sure that your landing area is devoid of trees.

There are many radical tricks to learn as a snowboarder. I can't describe all of them, or all of the lingo, here. However, if you hang out on the slopes or around the halfpipe, you will meet other snowboarders, and observing them will help you understand how the advanced tricks are practiced and performed. You might want to consider taking lessons from a certified PSIA instructor.

7. COMPETITIVE SNOWBOARDING

Snowboarding competitions began soon after the first snowboards were made. The Snurfer competitions in the northeast were sponsored by the Jem Corporation, makers of the Snurfer board.

The usual terrain was a smooth slope and the competitors would rip down this glassy run to see how fast they could get to the finish line. Speed was the objective.

Years later, with further development of the snowboard and its bindings, competition organizers began forming divisions to make the competitions fair. Divisions were formed for slalom, downhill, and freestyle riding.

Later, the halfpipe was developed. This type of competitive riding is similar to skateboard halfpipe competitions. A snowboarding halfpipe—it looks like a section of a pipe that is cut in half—is cut into a slope so that one end is higher than the other. This allows the rider to gain some speed so he can perform tricks off of the walls. This is a very dynamic form of the sport. There are many tricks that can be performed in the halfpipe that cannot be done freeriding.

It takes a very aggressive personality to be a halfpipe snowboarding competitor. Crashes are not unusual, so it takes a lot of

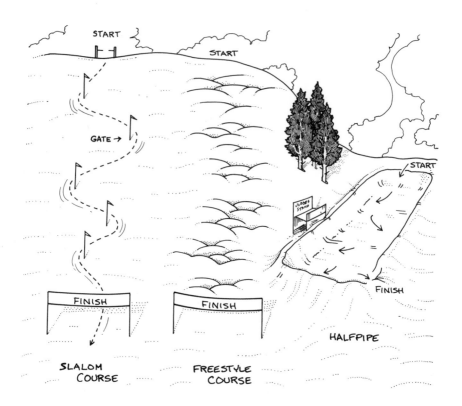

Figure 7-1   Competition courses

determination to become a good halfpipe rider. One of the best halfpipe riders in the United States is Damian Sanders.

I talked to Damian and found out what it takes to become a great halfpipe rider:

"Damian, when did you start snowboarding, and who or what turned you on to the sport?"
"In 1983 my brother Chris started a new company called Avalanche, which manufactures snowboards. He gave me the first board made by Avalanche."

"Did you have any idols as a beginner? Who inspired you the most?"
"In the early days my idols were skateboarders, people like Cristian Hosoi and Lester Kasai. The snowboarder I emulate is Terry Kidwell, he's better than everyone. My idols get big air."

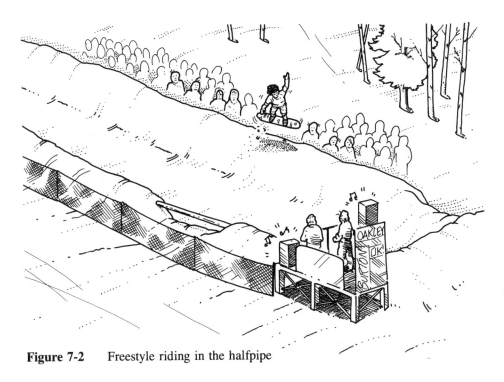

Figure 7-2   Freestyle riding in the halfpipe

"How did you get involved in competitive snowboarding?"
"When I started competing there were only a hundred or so competitors, you had a good chance of winning. I've been competing ever since."

"Do you compete in any events besides the halfpipe?"
"No, I only compete in freestyle competitions."

"Are you interested in any other sports?"
"Yes. I enjoy skateboarding, surfing, and riding motorcycles."

"What is it that motivates you to be so radical in the pipe or on the slopes?"
"I get no thrill (adrenaline rush) when my board is on the ground. The higher I get, the more of a rush the sport is."

"What steps do you take when you are learning a new trick?"
"Before I go to the halfpipe, I run through the trick many times in my mind. I visualize every move I'm going to make from the time I leave the jump until I land. Then I actually try the trick in the pipe. I try it over and over again until I make it."

"Do you think snowboarding equipment can be improved? If so, what development do you foresee in the future?"
"Yes, I have many ideas for the improvement of boots and bindings. Step in bindings and combination soft boots will be improved in the future."

"When is your next competition? What do you do to prepare yourself for a big event?"
"The competition season starts early next year. To prepare for a competition I free ride and then right before the event I practice in the half pipe."

"What will you do after you stop competing? Will you continue to be involved in the sport?"
"After I stop competing I want to be more involved with product development. I have a lot of ideas to work on."

"Do you have any advice you would like to give anyone wanting to get into competitive snowboarding?"
"Yea, don't rush it. Have fun snowboarding just for fun. If you feel you must compete, prepare yourself for a lot of upset."

8. BACKCOUNTRY SNOWBOARDING

Snowboarder's have started to leave the halfpipe competitions and resorts to explore the potential of their sport in the backcountry. Combining snowboarding with other sports, such as backcountry skiing and mountaineering, snowboarders have found a means to transport themselves to the most exciting runs imaginable.

Avalanche Danger

Get to know snow conditions. Avalanches are a serious problem in the backcountry, and the more you know about snow, the safer you will be. If you intend to board in an avalanche-prone area, you should always board with a group and wear a Pieps transmitter. A Pieps is a radio device that transmits and receives radio signals, and if you should get caught in an avalanche, your rescue will be initiated faster if you are wearing one. Many ski resorts and backcountry outfitters offer seminars on avalanche awareness and rescue.

Backcountry Equipment

When traveling into the backcountry, you will need some equipment for snow travel and safety. It's a good idea to carry a good backpack with an ice axe, a small first aid kit, a compass, extra clothing, sunblock, protein bars, a shovel, and a water bottle.

Figure 8-1   Backcountry snowboarding requires extensive knowledge of mountaineering skills.

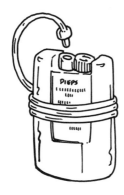 

Figure 8-2   Pieps radio/transmitter **Figure 8-3**   Backcountry equipment

The backpack should have enough room to carry your board and gear. Snowshoes are good to have. You may need them for climbing or traversing a slope. Collapsible ski poles are not essential, but they do come in handy on the flats or while hiking. Also, carry a space blanket and a flashlight or headlamp if you are going to be out after dark.

Two of the most experienced backcountry snowboarders in the United States are Jim Zellers and Bonnie Learey. Their adventures have taken them to Alaska, the Palasades, Patagonia, and many other mountainous areas of the world.

The following is an interview with these explorers:

"When did you start snowboarding?"
Jim, "In 1978."
"How about you Bonnie?"
"I started in 1985."

"Why did you stop competing?"
Jim, "I stopped competing after the 1988 world championships."
Bonnie, "Most competitions were unorganized and unprofessional ie. biased toward the sponsors' rider. It was a lot of work for a small return. I enjoy snowboarding more than standing around watching others, waiting for my turn.

"What is it that you enjoy most about backcountry snowboarding?"
Bonnie, "The backcountry!"

Jim, "I enjoy the lack of structured rules. The fact that I have to depend on myself or my partners. Everything is "open," and I don't have to deal with so many people."

"Do you think backcountry snowboarding is more dangerous than any other form of the sport?"
Bonnie, "Not more dangerous, just many more factors to consider. Mountaineering knowledge is required. Help is a long ways away.
Jim, "In the backcountry I'm a little more conservative because of the distance to help. I push it hard at the ski areas to improve my backcountry performance. In the backcountry I'm usually at 70 percent, so I need to up my 100 percent performance at the ski area to make my 70 percent higher."

"If someone asked you how to prepare for backcountry snowboarding, what would you recommend?"
Jim, "To prepare for the backcountry, I suggest some wilderness, snow, or climbing courses. There are a lot of schools around the country to teach the basics of the backcountry. In Lake Tahoe the Alpine Skills Institute has offered the first ever course combining snowboarding and the backcountry."

"Do you think the sport will develop more? What developments do you foresee?"
Jim, "The sport will constantly be developing in the near future. The biggest development will be total acceptance. Others will soon be aware that snowboarding is the ultimate sliding tool with no other function than fun! A generation will grow up and a large diverse group will be riding. Snowboards will change slightly, but the big development will be with boots and bindings. Eventually there will be a step-in system with a flexible boot."
Bonnie, "There will always be a "backcountry" faction. It will never be as big as the resort faction but I feel as more people are introduced into it by friends they will pick it up. I think crossover sports will develop: randanee' and climbing.

"What are some of the challenges that you look forward to in the future?"
Bonnie, "I would like to do a snowboard descent of Mt. Aspiring in New Zealand, and some Sierra descents."

Jim, "I look forward to really pushing the limits of steep descents and adventure snowboarding. I would like to set a precedent in steep descents and hopefully inspire others to do the real rad stuff. Things I'll never do. Specific challenges would be peaks in the Himilayas, Alaska, and in the Canadian Arctic. However, I would spend a lifetime in the Sierras on nameless peaks and chutes, which is what I bet I'll end up doing for the rest of my life."

"How long do you think you will continue to snowboard?"
Bonnie, "Always."
Jim, "I will continue snowboarding until by grandkids carry me off the hill and they take my board away."

9. ETHICS AND SAFETY

The sport of snowboarding has not always been accepted as it is now. In fact, it is still not allowed at some ski resorts. All ski areas enforce a skier's responsibility code. If a skier does not comply with the code, they may lose their pass or be asked to leave the area. Snowboarders must obey the code also. Since the sport is new to the resorts, we snowboarders must realize that the impression we make now will determine whether or not snowboarding will be allowed to continue at resorts.

Skier's Responsibility Code

1. Ski under control and in such a manner that you can stop or avoid other skiers or objects.

Translation:

Ski at your ability level.

Don't attempt jumps that are over your ability level.

Never jump where you are not absolutely certain that the landing area is clear.

Have a friend spot you below a jump.

Make sure your equipment is in good shape, and that it fits.

Safety leashes, metal edges, and supportive boots and bindings are required.

2. When skiing downhill or overtaking another skier, you
must avoid the skier below you.

3. You must not stop where you obstruct a trail or are not
visible from above.

Translation:

Move out of the way when you get off the lift and when
putting on your bindings.

When you stop, always come in on the downhill side of other
skiers.

Do not stop at an intersection, on a blind corner, on the
downside of a jump, or under a chair lift.

If you sit down to rest or to fasten your binding, do so to the
side of the trail.

4. When entering a trail or starting downhill, yield to other
skiers.

Translation:

Check uphill and peripherally when cutting across a run.

Follow these rules and maybe someday all ski areas will allow
us to enjoy their resort areas.

Some resorts have built halfpipes for freestyle riders. These
halfpipes usually have rules posted on the sides of the pipe. For
example, I have the list of rules for the halfpipe at Crested Butte
Ski Resort in Crested Butte, Colorado.

Halfpipe Rules:

Halfpipe users should make a reasonable visual inspection
prior to entering halfpipe and will be held to have assumed
the risk in using halfpipe.

Black Diamond
1. Snowboards only.
2. No inverted aerials.
3. Only two snowboarders allowed in halfpipe at one time.
4. Lift ticket required.
5. Halfpipe closed daily 10:30 A.M. to 12:00 P.M. for ski school classes.

Remember, your actions at a resort are a reflection of the actions of all snowboarders. If you are not obeying the rules, it could cause the sport and all its participants to lose the right to use the area.

APPENDIX A

Glossary

Air: When your snowboard leaves the ground. Many tricks can be performed in the air.

ABS: A strong plastic used for the deck material in the construction of a snowboard.

Aluminum: A light-weight metal commonly used in the construction of snowboards. Stronger than fiberglass, aluminum provides better damping.

Amped: Really psyched to rage!

Angle: The angle of the feet on the board.

Asymmetrical: This term applies to boards with shifted sidecuts, where the overall shape is designed for one stance, regular or goofy.

Backside: The same as heelside. The side of the halfpipe that is facing the back of the rider is referred to as the backside wall.

Bail: The method of attaching a plate binding to the boot. A metal bail on the front attaches to the welt of the boot; a plastic bail in the back is set into the rear welt and clamped on. This grips the boot between the bails.

Base grade: This is the bottom layer of material on a snowboard.

Bevel: The degree of angle the base has by its edge.

Binding: The mechanism used to connect the rider's boots to the board.

Bogged: When a rider is slowed by deep snow.

Boned: Boned out, or boning, refers to a straight leg move.

Camber: The amount of arch in the board when you put it flat on the floor.

Cant: The amount of angle that either foot is tilted toward the other.

Carbon fiber graphite: A light-weight material used in the construction of snowboards. Similar to fiberglass, but stronger. It comes in a cloth form, which is layered into the board.

Carve: Carving a turn refers to the act of turning the board without sliding.

Clogging: When a run is blocked by other snowboarders or skiers.

Core materials: The core of the board is material that determines the board's shape and flex pattern.

Cornice: An overhang formed by wind along the edge or top of a snowy ridge.

Couloir: A steep section of snow or ice that forms in a gully on a mountain.

Crampon: A crampon is made of metal and shaped like the sole of a boot. It has spikes on the bottom and is made for climbing on ice or snow. It is attached to a boot by straps or a step in binding.

Damping: A reduction in the chatter and vibration of the snowboard.

Drop: Jumping off a cornice or cliff.

Dual slalom: A slalom race involving two riders racing at the same time.

Edge: The metal edge which runs completely around the base on the bottom of the board.

Effective edge: The length of the edge that is in contact with the snow during a turn.

Extruded base: Polyethylene is melted and pressed through a form to make the base.

Fakie: When a rider's rear foot is forward to the direction of travel.

Fall Line: An imaginary line down the slope. The path that a falling object will take.

Fiberglass: Epoxy resin and layers of glass-fiber cloth are used to construct this material for many snowboards.

Flex: How easily the board bends.

Frontside: The side of the board that the rider faces. Same as the toeside.

Half-cab: A freeriding maneuver where the rider approaches a bump fakie, gets air, does a 180-degree spin, and lands in a regular forward position.

Halfpipe: A section of snow either natural or man-made that looks like a pipe that has been cut in half lengthwise.

Hand-plant: An aerial move with the rider touching the lip of the pipe.

Hardpack: A snow condition where the snow is groomed, then packed to leave a very hard surface.

Heelside: Refers to the edge of the board under the heel of the rider.

Insert: A threaded nut that is in the board so you can mount the bindings to the board without drilling holes.

Invert: An aerial maneuver where the rider is upside down and is not touching the lip of the pipe. Way rad!

Line: The route a rider chooses to take.

Mogul: The crisscross turning patterns of downhill skiers leaves a field of bumps on the hill. These bumps are called moguls.

Mounting plate: An aluminum or other reinforced plate in the board so bindings can be screwed directly to it.

Nose: The width of the board at the widest part of the nose. The front of the board.

Pieps: A radio device worn by skiers who are skiing in an avalanche-prone area. Enables rescuers to locate and to retrieve a buried party quickly.

Polyurethane: Polyurethane, or foam, is commonly used as a core material because of its durability and low cost.

Post-holing: Walking in deep snow without snowshoes or skis.

Powder: A large accumulation of dry snow.

PSIA: Professional Ski Instructors of America.

P-Tex: A stick form of polyurethane used to fill the cuts in the base of skis or snowboards.

Rad: Short for radical. Something wild or crazy might be called Rad.

Rail slide: A rail is a section of wood, usually a post, positioned on the lip of a halfpipe. A rider will use the rail to perform a trick, such as the rail slide.

Raging: Having a good day or going fast.

Ripped: A perfectly executed maneuver.

Roll-out deck: The area of a halfpipe where a rider finishes and exits the pipe.

Run: A prepared area. Designed for skiing or snowboarding. Usually given a name and rating of difficulty.

Shred: When a rider is having a great time, or a perfect day!

Sidecut: The difference between the waistwidth and the nose and tailwidths. There are several types of curves used in shaping sidecuts: radial, elliptical, quadratic, and progressive.

Sideslip: A basic maneuver performed facing uphill or downhill while the board is flat on the snow and perpendicular to the slope.

Sintered base: Polyethylene is ground into particles, then is heated and pressed together under high pressure.

Sketch: When a rider is about to crash.

Slalom: A downhill race. A course of obstacles, called gates, are positioned down a hill. The rider goes from side to side around the gates. Two identical courses are set side by side, and riders race against each other and against a clock.

Snow cat: An oversnow vehicle used to transport people and equipment to hard-to-reach areas.

Stance: Refers to the rider's position on the board. A "Regular" stance is left foot forward on the board. A "Goofy" stance is right foot forward.

Super G: The giant slalom, longer than a slalom race. The race-course is wider and often has jumps.

Swing weight: This is a measure of the tendency of the board to resist rotation (or, rotational inertia).

Tail: The widest point at the back of the board.

Tailing arm: The rider's back arm.

Taper angle: This is the difference between the width of the nose and tail.

Terrain: Bumps, trees, steeps, groomed, crud, ice, banks, slush, crust, and powder are snowboarding terrains.

Thickness: Most boards have a variable thickness, thinner at the nose and tail, thicker at the waist. This gives the board a graduated flex. Cheap boards come with a constant thickness.

Toeside: Refers to the edge of the board under the toes of the rider.

Tweak: When the board is pulled to the front or pushed to the back of the rider while in the air.

Waist: The narrowest point in the middle of the board.

Width: The distance between the front foot and back foot is the stance width. Width may refer to the width of the board at the waist.

Wipeout: A crash or hard fall.

Wood laminate: Wood is commonly used as a core material. Wood laminate cores come in two configurations: vertical and horizontal.

INDEX